SUSHI

TABLE OF CONTENTS

There's no stopping the cultivation of the art of the appetizer. Spoil yourself and your guests with sushi, it's easier to make than you think. Once you have tried this delicious gourmet treat, you are sure to become an enthusiast.

The classics of Japanese cuisine

Sushi has become synonymous with Japanese cuisine, the three principles of which are nature, harmony, and esthetics. Nature refers to the attempt to leave the food as unaltered as possible during preparation in order to retain its natural flavor as well as using mainly seasonal produce. Harmony signifies the combination of ingredients as far as taste, texture, and color is concerned. Esthetics aims at the most elegant arrangement and decoration. What appears to be elaborate and exotic to westerners may be considered not unusual in Japan.

Even today, despite the high-tech lifestyle and fast-food culture, the people of the Land of the Rising Sun cultivate a traditional cuisine and regard food as a work of art in its own right.

More than just a trend

There has been a real boom in Sushi in the West in recent years. There are so many sushi bars around, even small cities can claim to have one. More and more curious eaters overcome their objections to raw fish and discover the pleasure of this new taste experience.

Apart from the tender and delicate fish, you can fill or garnish sushi with other steamed ingredients, such as vegetables and eggs. The possibilities with the various sushi types are extremely varied. Sushi has been transformed from an exclusive snack only accessible to a small circle of gourmets to delicious food for everyone.

In a restaurant or bar, however, sushi is far from being a bargain. That is why more and more sushi enthusiasts are daring to make sushi at home. With a little dexterity and patience, the results will both be beautiful and tasty.

The recipes in this book are so detailed that even an inexperienced sushi cook can be sure of success. "Did you really do this all by yourself?" your guests are bound to ask, since what you serve them will look perfectly formed.

Healthy & figure-friendly

Nutritionists are full of praise for sushi as a balanced and especially healthy food because it is immensely nutritious as well as being very low fat. Fish and seafood provide the full spectrum of nutrients. All the ingredients promote mental and physical fitness, consisting as they do of high-quality proteins, vitamins, minerals, and the essential omega-3 acids. Rice and vegetables are

5

important sources of complex carbohydrate and fiber. Nori is pressed seaweed and contains unusually high amounts of minerals and vitamins, especially iodine and vitamin B_{12}. This should be of great interest to vegetarians, as this is the only source of vitamin B_{12} other than in animal foods. All in all, eating sushi will benefit both your health and your figure.

How should you eat sushi?

Every Japanese person is served sushi with a small saucer for the Japanese type of soy sauce, which is also known as shoyu. You can add a little wasabi, a green horseradish paste.

Thin pink strips of pickled ginger neutralize and freshen the palate before the next bite.

The same effect can be obtained from a sip of miso soup (recipe page 15), green tea, or water. You should usually put the whole sushi roll into your mouth after dipping it in the sauce. Do not try to bite off a piece—you will fail! Only Temaki Sushi can be enjoyed bite by bite.

With Nigiri, Hoso Maki, and Uru Maki Sushi as well as Gunkan Maki you have the choice of using chopsticks or your fingers, as they are eaten in both ways in Japan. Knives and forks on the other hand are absolutely taboo. Temaki Sushi is always eaten with the fingers. Sashimi, Chirashi, and steamed Sushi are traditionally eaten with chopsticks. If you really get into difficulties, then you may have to resort to using a fork.

6

Appetizers, Rolls, Cylinders, Cones

Nigiri Sushi
The original form of sushi consisted of fish on top and rice underneath. Fish, shrimp, etc are basted with wasabi paste and pressed onto a shaped clump of rice. Nigiri Sushi is always served two at a time.

Maki Sushi Rolls
The filling is on the inside, surrounded by rice, and the whole thing is wrapped in seaweed. In the small Hosomaki rolls there are one or two ingredients in the filling and one roll is divided into six pieces. The thick Futo Maki rolls contain three to five filling ingredients and are usually cut into eight slices.

Gunkan Maki
Small molds with a soft filling: rice is used as the base and a piece of seaweed is wrapped round the rice. This can be filled with fish roe and other bulky or chopped ingredients.

Temaki
Small cones are fashioned from seaweed. These are filled with sushi rice and other ingredients.

Ura Maki
"Inside out" rolls with a filling in the middle, followed by seaweed and rice outside, thus the opposite way around to standard sushi.

Sashimi
Sushi without rice: raw pieces of raw, filleted fish with vegetables are arranged skillfully on plates or sushi boards.

Chirashi
Mostly warm Sushi rice in a bowl, with various other ingredients, usually including fish.

Essential Ingredients

You will find these typically Japanese ingredients in the Asian foods section of good supermarkets and, of course, in any Asian grocery store.

Above (from left to right):

Nori sheets: Made from dried and pressed seaweed. The green, paper-thin sheets are used for wrapping Maki Sushi and Temaki Sushi. It is best to buy them ready toasted.

Sushi Rice: This special rice is best suited for making sushi, as it is sticky after cooking and therefore especially easy to shape. If you have to use a substitute, use round-grain or Carolina rice. Non-sticky, long grain rice varieties or precooked rice are quite unsuitable for sushi.

Sesame seeds: The light-colored seeds are usually roasted and used as an aromatic seasoning; black sesame seeds are used mainly as a garnish.

Shiitake Mushrooms: Also known under the Chinese name of *tongu*. The dried forms are more spicy than fresh. Make sure that fresh mushrooms have fleshy caps that are undamaged.
Simmer the mushrooms in a spicy broth and use them either as fillings or as a wrapping.

Kombu: A type of seaweed that is easy to find in oriental and healthfood stores. It is sold dried in thick sheets and is used as a sushi ingredient.

Kampyo: Long thin strips of dried pumpkin. After soaking it, simmer it in broth until soft and use as a filling or wrapping.

Above (in the bottles, from left to right):
Sake: Japanese rice wine. Both the national drink and an important ingredient in the cuisine.
Rice vinegar (su): Used for flavoring the rice. Japanese rice vinegar is very mild. >>

Typical Tools

These are the most important kitchen utensils for sushi preparation. Specialist tools, though not necessary, make preparation easier. You will probably be able to find substitutes for those you cannot find. However, if you are serious about sushi-making you will find everything you need in Asian grocery stores.

>>
Alternatively, use a very diluted fruit vinegar.
Mirin: Sweet rice wine, only used as a seasoning. You can use Amontillado sherry as a substitute.
Soy sauce: The Japanese all-purpose seasoning, which may be salty or slightly sweet. Use the dark, salty variety for sushi.
Dashi: Fish broth, here an instant variety.

The bowls with the bottles, facing page, contain:
Wasabi: Extremely hot green horseradish. It is available as a ready-made paste or as a powder, which hast to be mixed with water.
Pickled ginger (shoga): These thin slices stay fresh for weeks if kept in a cool place.

Above (from bottom to top):
Chopping board: Choose a large, stable one.
Wooden spatula: Makes it easier to stir the vinegar mixture into the rice.
Kitchen knife: Should be extremely sharp. It has a long, thin blade for slicing fish very accurately, and a broad blade for cutting vegetables and other ingredients.
Cooking skewers: For stirring ingredients (alternatively use, a spoon or a fork).
Tweezers: For removing stray fishbones.
Wooden bowl (hangiri): Useful, as it absorbs any excess sogginess of the rice.
You can also use a wooden, unlacquered salad bowl or earthenware bowl.
Fans: Fanning the rice cools it quicker.
Bamboo rolling mat (makisu): Used for shaping the sushi rolls.
Bamboo-baskets: The stackable ones are perfect for steaming Mushi Sushi.

Nigiri Sushi

"Nigiri" means "to press" because the topping has to be pressed into the rice to make this attractive type of sushi. There are four different traditional shapes into which sushi rice is shaped. You will probably not need to master any more than the cylindrical form, which is the one that is used the most in this book.

1 For a fish topping—tuna, in this case—slice each fillet as evenly as possible crosswise across the grain at a slight angle, to make eight thin slices around 1 x 2 inches in size.

2 Use your fingertip to spread a little wasabi paste over the center of one side of each of the fish slices. Wet your hands and shape the rice into eight cylinders.

3 If you are right-handed, place a slice of fish, wasabi paste side upward, in your left palm. Place a cylinder of rice on top and press it down with your thumb. The rice and fish should now stick together firmly.

4 Take the sushi in the other hand, while turning it and press the topping against the rice. Return the sushi to your left hand and press the long side gently with your right thumb and index finger to mold it into a cylindrical shape. Repeat the last two steps once or twice more.

5 Now re-shape the sushi with the index finger of your right hand, squeezing gently from top to bottom, to create the typically rounded shape.

Maki Sushi

Maki Sushi, also known as Hosomaki Sushi, consists of rice, spread with a filling and rolled inside half a sheet of nori. The thicker Futo Maki are made using a whole sheet of nori. Place half a sheet of nori, smooth side downward, in the center of a bamboo rolling mat, with one long side against the edge of the mat.

1 Rinse your hands in vinegar water. Cover the sheet of nori with a layer of rice at room temperature, but do not cover the edges of the nori on the longest sides. The layer should not be more than ½ inch thick. Do not press down too firmly.

2 Place fillings in the center of the rice. They should be at room temperature, except for fish, which should be chilled. Lift the mat at the short end closest to you, and roll it up around the nori. Just before you complete the rolling action, pull away the end of the mat so it does not get caught in the sushi.

3 To make the roll into its final shape, place part of the bamboo mat over the roll and press gently. Remove the mat. Place the roll, seam downward, on a wooden board. Lightly press the open ends to keep the mixture firm. Take a large, sharp knife that has been dipped in vinegar water and cut the roll in half.

4 Place the two halves of the sushi roll next to each other and divide them into two or three more rolls each, depending on the recipe. You can slice them vertically or on the diagonal. This will give you four larger or six small rolls. Arrange the Maki Sushi decoratively on a platter, cut sides upward.

11

Gunkan Maki

This variety of sushi is composed of fillings of a soft consistency, such as salmon roe as in this example, held in place by a "wall" of strips of nori.

1 Moisten your hands and shape eight long, oval clumps of the sushi rice. Wrap a piece of nori around each clump of rice, smooth side upward. Stick one or two rice grains on the bottom of the strip ends and press them into the nori sheet with it.

2 Press the rice carefully each time into the nori sheet and spread whatever filling is used in the recipe evenly over it. Garnish the Gunkan Maki.

Ura Maki Sushi

This type of "counter-clockwise rolled" sushi needs great care when being shaped, but it is visually very appealing.

1 Cover a bamboo roll-mat with plastic wrap and moisten it a little to avoid rice sticking to it. If you don't have a proper bamboo sushi mat use extra-strong aluminum foil. You won't have to cover it with plastic wrap but it should be moistened with vinegar water.

2 Put half a nori sheet, smooth side down, on the bamboo mat so that the long bottom edge covers the bamboo mat.

3 Moisten your hands with vinegar water. Cover the nori sheet with a layer of less than half an inch of warm sushi rice, making sure you don't press the rice too hard and crush it. Leave a small bare margin along sides.

4 Turn the nori sheet filled with rice so that the rice is now underneath. Squeeze or paint a thin stripe of mayonnaise along the middle of the nori sheet and distribute the filling evenly on top.

5 Form a roll with the mat and press together as described for Maki Sushi. Cut the roll in half with a sharp knife dipped in vinegar water. Then place both halves next to each other and cut them in three to obtain six pieces of sushi. Dip each in toasted sesame seeds and arrange with the cut surface upward.

Temaki Sushi

Temaki Sushi is rolled using either half a nori sheet into bigger or a quarter of a sheet into smaller "cones."

1 Form four to eight small balls from the sushi rice, using moistened hands. Place the nori sheet, smooth side downward, into your left palm.

2 Place a ball of rice at the top end of the nori sheet. Use a fingertip to smear it with a tiny amount of wasabi paste. Place a quarter or an eighth of the filling, which in this case is salmon, cucumber, and radish, onto the rice and press lightly so that the nori sheet, rice, and filling stick together.

3 Roll the nori sheet with the filling into a cone, which is slightly pointed at the bottom so that the contents can't escape. Stick the nori sheet to the scone with one or two rice grains.

13

Three things must always accompany sushi: soy sauce, wasabi paste, and pickled ginger but a few light side-dishes are often served as well.

Sweet-and-sour Vegetable Strips
Serves four

Ingredients
4 oz (each) white radish, carrots, and cucumber
1 tbsp salt
1 piece untreated lemon peel
5 tbsp rice vinegar
3 tbsp sugar
1 tsp freshly grated ginger

Wash, peel, and slice the vegetables into 1-inch long, matchstick strips. Mix with salt and leave for 10 minutes. Rinse well in fresh water and squeeze. Slice the lemon peel into paper-thin strips. Boil the vinegar with sugar, the lemon peel, and ginger and pour this over the vegetables. Marinate for at least one hour, stirring occasionally. If covered, the strips will keep for five days in the refrigerator.

Spinach Salad with Sesame Dressing
Serves four

Ingredients
4 cups leaf spinach
salt
2 tsp peeled sesame seeds
2 tbsp sesame paste (in a jar)
2 tbsp light soy sauce
2 tbsp dashi (instant fish broth) or water
½ tbsp sugar

Clean, wash, and blanch the spinach in boiling salted water for one minute. Drain in a sieve, rinse with cold water, and drain well. Toast the sesame seeds in a dry frying pan. Stir the sesame paste into the soy sauce, with the dashi or water and add sugar. Dip the spinach in the sauce; add salt to taste and sprinkle with sesame seeds.

Miso soup with Tofu

Serves four

Ingredients
1 quart dashi (instant fish broth)
2 scallions
1 scant cup firm tofu
⅓ cup miso (soybean paste)
1 tbsp sake (Japanese rice wine)
salt

Bring the dashi to the boil. Wash the scallions and slice them crosswise into paper-thin stripes. Dice the tofu. Stir a little of the broth into the miso and pour it with the sake into the rest of the liquid, stirring to prevent the formation of lumps. Cook the tofu and onions for five minutes in the liquid and add salt to taste.

Which drinks go with Sushi?

The traditional drink to accompany Japanese food is green tea. Its subtle taste harmonizes particularly well with sushi, as opposed to black tea which would taste too bitter. Sake, a rice wine, is also a classic accompaniment. It comes in small bottles, and is first warmed in hot water before being drunk from tiny porcelain bowls. On hot days, it may also be drunk ice cold. Beer, both Japanese and American, is also a favorite with sushi. Spring water is, of course, an option.

Sushi Rice

To make 3 pounds ready-cooked sushi rice

1 Wash the sushi rice under running water until the water runs clear. Drain off the water and pour the rice and 3 cups water into a shallow, heavy-based pan; add the piece of kombu. Let the rice soak and swell for at least 10 minutes.

2 Bring the rice to the boil, stirring occasionally, and let it cook for 2 minutes on high heat. Then reduce the heat to a minimum and let the rice swell according to the cooking instructions on the package for another 10–20 minutes. The rice should be just cooked.

3 In the meantime, beat the rice vinegar with salt and sugar in a small bowl, using an egg whisk, until they are well combined.

4 Remove sushi rice from the cooker, take the lid off, cover the rice with a kitchen towel, and leave it to cool for another 10 minutes; it will continue to swell. Take a Japanese wooden bowl (hangiri) or other shallow bowl made of unlacquered wood or earthenware and rinse it with cold water. Pour the cooked rice into it.

5 Turn the rice quickly with a flat wooden spatula and sprinkle the vinegar mixture over it.

6 In order to cool the rice quickly to room temperature as well as ensure it is not too sticky and is shiny, make furrows as with a plow, using the wooden spatula, going from left to right and from top to bottom. Make sure you do not stir it and don't crush the grains. In between, supply some air to the rice with a fan or by fanning it with the wooden spatula. The cooling and loosening of the rice takes about 10 minutes (you must never put the rice into the refrigerator to cool it off.)

7 Cover the sushi rice with a damp kitchen towel so that it doesn't dry out, and use as suggested in the recipes.

For use in Chirashi Sushi and Mushi Sushi (steamed sushi), add rice vinegar and salt to taste.

This amount of rice can be used for each of the following:
3 servings of Nigiri Sushi,
1 serving of Hosomaki Sushi,
1 serving of Futo Maki and
1 serving of Temaki Sushi

Or one of the following:
1 serving of Hosomaki Sushi,
1 serving of Gunkan Maki and
1 serving of Chirashi or steamed sushi.

Both combinations are plenty for 4–6 people.

NIGIRI SUSHI
Culinary Miniatures

It is simply fascinating watching a **Japanese sushi chef** preparing Nigiri Sushi behind the counter, with fast and incredibly elegant movements. But don't despair! With a little **perseverance and patience** anyone can at least achieve the status of an **amateur sushi-maker.**

The archetypal sushi

Sushi has featured in Japanese literature for many centuries. In the past, only fish and shell-fish were called "sushi" and were pickled to preserve them. Over time, rice was added which greatly improved the flavor of the fish.

In the nineteenth century, the archetype of today's Nigiri Sushi appeared. Peddlars would put a slice of raw fish on a finger-long clump of rice moistened with vinegar and offered the bites as simple and inexpensive street food. Sushi was packed in little boxes and carried home. But times have changed, sushi is no longer a part of the everyday diet—it's now something infinitely more sophisticated and expensive, a treat for special occasions.

The sushi varieties

Whether in Japan or abroad, when people talk of sushi they mostly mean Nigiri Sushi. But there is a good array of different varieties from all of the islands of which Japan consists. Only a small fraction are created in the sushi bars of the West, where hand-made Nigiri are both the most popular and the favorite variety. As a starter, two pieces per person is considered adequate, but eaten as an entrée, eight to ten pieces should suffice.

The pleasure starts with buying the fish

For the preparation of sushi you don't normally need a lot of ingredients but everything must be of the finest and freshest. This is especially true if you are using raw fish in a layer or as a filling. Tell your fishmarket that you intend to eat the fish raw and use the term "fillet of sushi quality". A very fresh fish fillet has firm flesh that gives when pressed with the finger. It slices smoothly and the slices have a pearly sheen. The flesh must never be flabby or yellowish. A really fresh fish fillet never smells strongly of fish, but has a fragrance that is redolent of the sea. It is best to buy the fish on the day on which you are going to prepare sushi. In an exceptional case, such as over the weekend, you can store it for a day in the refrigerator, wrapped in aluminum foil. When using frozen fish or shellfish, remove them from the package, place on a plate, cover, and leave to defrost in the refrigerator. Then rinse briefly and dry it with a cloth.

Tips & Tricks for preparation

In theory, Nigiri Sushi is supposed to be the simplest version of sushi.

In practice, however, the situation is a little different. A Japanese sushi cook has to train for years before he or she is to serve this specialty like a master.

But don't worry, yet—with a little practice anyone can make and serve attractive sushi. The way to shape sushi is described step-by-step on page 10. You should ensure that the raw fish doesn't get warm while you are shaping the sushi. Ideally, you should eat sushi a few minutes after it has been been made. This isn't a problem in a sushi bar, but it's not always possible at home. You can prepare Nigiri Sushi up to two hours before serving. Cover the prepared sushi with plastic wrap and store in the refrigerator. It should just be at room temperature when served.

Arrangement & presentation

Arranging sushi in Japan is an art form with strict rules. At home, you can be more relaxed about it. Traditionally, Nigiri Sushi should be served in pairs for each person and the selection should display as many colors as possible. Thus "red" for example can be represented by red tuna, "white" by any white fish varieties such as sea-bass or bream. You will get "blue" from the bluish skin of mackerel and sardines. The "orange" color is represented by salmon and "yellow" by the eel and by omelets.

Eating Nigiri Sushi

Those who are skilled at handling chopsticks put the Nigiri Sushi at the side of the plate and pick it up in such a way that the top layer can be dipped in the soy sauce—spiced with wasabi paste to taste. Do not dip the rice side in the sauce, as it will make the rice crumbly. Do not pour soy sauce over the sushi either. If you prefer to eat Nigiri Sushi with your fingers, the best way is to place the index finger at the end of the top layer and grasp the piece of sushi with the thumb and the middle finger. This way, it can be easily lifted and dipped in the soy sauce.

*6 oz very fresh tuna
("otoro," "chutoro," or "akami," see Tip on this page)
2 tsp wasabi paste
⅔ cup prepared sushi rice
(recipe page 16)*

For dipping and accompaniments
*soy sauce • wasabi paste
shredded pickled ginger*

Time *25 minutes
60 calories per roll*

Nigiri Sushi with Tuna

8 pieces • Easy to make • A Classic

1 Pat the tuna flesh dry. Remove any remaining fishbones with tweezers. Trim any ragged sides. Cut the flesh as thinly and as evenly as possible against the grain into eight slices 1¼ x 2 inches each.

2 Spread one side of the fish slices with a little wasabi paste, using a fingertip. Shape the rice into eight longish clumps with moistened hands and prepare Nigiri Sushi as described on page 10. When ready, serve as soon as possible. ■

Tip

Tuna (maguro) is a classic sushi ingredient and also the favorite. Sushi beginners are often surprised that it tastes more like lean beef or veal, than fish. This depends, apart from variety of tuna used, on the part of the fish from which the pieces were cut. Besides the taste, the parts differ in color and price. In Japan, and in many sushi bars in the West, you can choose between three different parts of the fish. The lighter and fatter "otoro" flesh, cut out from the belly, is particularly appreciated in Japan. For connoisseurs nowadays it's the first choice and therefore expensive accordingly. "Chutoro" is also cut from the belly area. The flesh is leaner and is medium-red in color. "Akami," the tuna part around the center bones, on the other hand, is dark red and lean. Try them all to find which you like best.

Ingredients

8 raw peeled jumbo shrimp tails (fresh or deep-frozen, each weighing about 1 oz)
salt • 2 tbsp rice vinegar
2 tbsp mirin (Japanese cooking sherry)
2 tsp wasabi paste
⅔ cup prepared sushi rice (recipe page 16)

Additionally: 8 metal or wooden kabob skewers

For dipping and accompaniments
soy sauce • wasabi paste
shredded pickled ginger

Time *30 minutes*
50 calories per piece

Nigiri Sushi with Shrimp

8 pieces • A little more expensive

1 Thread fresh or deep-frozen thawed shrimp onto a skewer. Cook in a boiling salted water on low heat for 3–4 minutes. Remove and rinse in ice-cold water.

2 Shell the shrimp. Devein them by cutting along the top with a sharp knife point. Slice the shrimp lengthwise with a knife point, to remove the thin, dark intestine. Slice them lengthwise, but don't cut right through, and open them up like a butterfly.

3 Mix rice vinegar with mirin. Marinate the prawns in it for three minutes, take them out and dry with a cloth. Daub the bottom sides thinly with wasabi paste.

4 Wet your hands and shape the sushi rice into eight cylindrical clumps. Prepare the Nigiri Sushi as described on page 10. ∎

Ingredients

6 oz really fresh salmon fillet
2 tsp wasabi paste
⅔ cup prepared sushi rice (recipe page 16)
2 tbsp salmon roe

For dipping and accompaniments
soy sauce • wasabi paste
shredded pickled ginger

Time *25 minutes*
60 calories per piece

Nigiri Sushi with Salmon

8 pieces • For entertaining

1 Cut the salmon fillet at a slight angle against the grain into eight paper-thin, even 1¼ x 2 inch slices. This is easier to do if the fillet is slightly frozen. To freeze, wrap the fish in aluminum foil and leave it into the freezer for around an hour.

2 When the salmon is defrosted but is still very cold, spread one side with a thin layer of wasabi paste. Wet your hands and shape the sushi rice into longish clumps, about 3 inches long.

Finish the Nigiri Sushi as described on page 10. Garnish with salmon roe, arrange, and serve as soon as possible. ∎

Tip

Connoisseurs will choose wild or organic salmon, the latter being farmed according to strict ecological rules. The fish are not fed any food supplements, hormones, or medications and so they have firm and incomparably tasty flesh.

**Nigiri Sushi
with Shrimp**

**Nigiri Sushi
with Salmon**

Ingredients

1 very fresh mackerel fillet
with skin (about 6 oz)
2 tbsp salt
3 tbsp rice vinegar
1 tbsp mirin (Japanese
cooking sherry)
1 tsp sugar
2 tsp wasabi paste
⅔ cup prepared sushi rice
(recipe page 16)
1 scallion
1 small piece fresh ginger
(about 1 oz)

For dipping and accompaniments
soy sauce • wasabi paste
shredded pickled ginger

Time 25 minutes (+ 5–6
hours resting time)
60 calories per piece

Nigiri Sushi with Mackerel

8 pieces • Spicy • Easy to make

1 Wash the mackerel fillet, pat dry with a cloth, and remove any remaining bones. Trim any ragged edges. Rub the fillet with salt, wrap it in plastic wrap, and let it rest in the refrigerator for 4–5 hours. Rinse the salt off the fish under running water and dry it with a cloth.

2 Place the mackerel fillet in a shallow bowl. Mix rice vinegar with the mirin and sugar until the sugar dissolves. Pour this marinade over the fillet, cover it, and let it soak for 30 minutes to one hour in the refrigerator, turning it once.

3 Remove the fillet from the marinade and dry it with a cloth. Remove the skin, separating some tail flesh from it with a sharp knife. Cut the mackerel fillet slightly at an angle into eight thick, even slices.

4 Spread one side of each slice with wasabi paste, using your fingertips. Shape the sushi rice into eight longish cylinders and prepare the Nigiri Sushi as described on page 10.

5 Rinse the scallions and slice them into paper-thin rings. Peel the ginger and grate or shred it very finely. Serve the sushi garnished with the scallion rings and ginger. ■

Variation
Nigiri Sushi with sardines

You can use this recipe to make sushi with fresh sardines. For this purpose, prepare one very fresh sardine fillet with the skin (around 5½ ounces) or eight fillets sliced like the mackerel fillet described above. Rub it with salt, let it rest for 15 minutes, then rinse and marinate for half an hour. In contrast to the mackerel, sardine sushi is served with the skin on. Use a sharp knife to slash the skin in parallel lines. This is not only decorative, but also makes an appetizing color contrast between the silvery skin of the sardine and its dark flesh.

Ingredients

4 tbsp soy sauce
⅓ cup mirin (Japanese cooking sherry)
1 tbsp sugar
1 raw eel (weighing about 1 lb 9 oz, filleted by the fishmonger, but with the bones)
oil for frying
1 tbsp sesame seeds
⅔ cup prepared sushi rice (recipe page 16)
2 tsp wasabi paste
1 toasted sheet of nori
8 long metal or wooden kabob skewers

For dipping and accompaniments

soy sauce • wasabi paste
shredded pickled ginger

Time *1½ hours*
235 calories per piece

Nigiri Sushi with Eel

8 pieces • A little more elaborate • Sophisticated

1 To make the eel sauce, blend the soy sauce with mirin and sugar in a wide pot. Wash and dry the eel bones, cut them into pieces, and add to the pot. Bring it to the boil and simmer, uncovered, for some 45 minutes on medium or low heat until the liquid thickens.

2 In the meantime, wash the eel flesh, dry them and remove any remaining fishbone. Cut the fillets depending on the length into pieces 4½–6 inches long and thread them onto a skewer. Fry the eel pieces for about two minutes on each side, either in hot oil in a pan, or place them side by side on a sheet of aluminum foil. Slide them under a preheated broiler and broil for 5–6 minutes, turning several times. Remove the skewers and drain the eel pieces off fat on kitchen paper.

3 Strain the eel sauce and remove 2 tablespoons of it. Place the fish on the aluminum foil again and brush repeatedly all over with the remaining sauce.

4 Toast the sesame seeds in a dry pan on medium heat until golden brown. Cut the nori sheet into eight strips. Shape the sushi rice into eight oval clumps and smear them with wasabi paste, using a fingertip.

5 Shape the eel pieces and the rice into Nigiri Sushi as described on page 10. Wrap a strip of nori around the middle of each piece of sushi and secure the ends together with a grain of rice. Brush the eel lightly with the remaining sauce and sprinkle with the sesame seeds. ■

Tips

• Eel bones add flavor to the sauce and will thicken it at the same time. If you can't use the bones, thicken the sauce with a little potato starch.
• Prepare more of the eel sauce than you need as it can also be used for seasoning tuna sushi. It will keep in the refrigerator for several weeks if stored in a screw-top jar.
• If you cannot get fresh eel, use smoked eel or smoked whitefish. Make the sauce from the bones and trimmings of other fish.

Ingredients

6 oz fresh sea-bass fillet
2 tsp wasabi paste
⅔ cup prepared sushi rice
(recipe page 16)
½–1 bunch of chives

For dipping and accompaniments
soy sauce • wasabi paste
shredded pickled ginger

Time *25 minutes*
40 calories per piece

Nigiri Sushi with Sea-bass

8 pieces • The sea-bass makes it special

1 Dry the sea bass fillet with a cloth and remove any remaining bones with tweezers. Trim away any ragged edges. Cut the flesh at an angle across the grain into eight paper-thin, even slices measuring about 1¼ x 2 inches.

2 Use a fingertip to spread the slices with wasabi paste and shape the sushi rice with moistened hands into eight cylindrical clumps. Prepare Nigiri Sushi as described on page 10.

3 Wash and dry the chives. Garnish the sushi pieces with a stem each and serve immediately. ■

Tip
Instead of sea bass you can prepare sushi with other white fish varieties such as plaice or porgy, and even with trout or other fresh water fish.

Ingredients

6–8 oz very fresh, prepared squid pouches
8 large, flat-leaved parsley leaves
2 tsp wasabi paste
⅔ cup prepared sushi rice
(recipe page 16)

For dipping and accompaniments
soy sauce • wasabi paste
shredded pickled ginger

Time *30 minutes*
35 calories per piece

Nigiri Sushi with Calamari

8 pieces • Easy to make

1 Cut the squid pouches down one side, wash and dry them with a cloth, roll them out flat and cut them into eight pieces, around ⅛ x ¼ inch each. Slash three 1⁄16-inch deep cuts down them with a sharp knife.

2 Wash the parsley leaves and dry them with a cloth. Spread the smooth side of the calamari thinly with wasabi paste and place a parsley leaf on top. Shape the sushi rice into eight cylindrical clumps

and prepare Nigiri Sushi from the rice and calamari as described on page 10. ■

Tip
If you don't like the idea of eating raw calamari you can cook them first. Just simmer the pouches in water on low heat for three minutes and slice them when cool.

Nigiri Sushi
with Sea-bass

Nigiri Sushi
with Calamari

Ingredients
8 very fresh anchovies
2 tbsp salt
1 piece of ginger the size of
a walnut
5 tbsp rice vinegar
2 tbsp mirin
2 tsp sugar
2 tsp wasabi powder
acidulated water
⅔ cup prepared sushi rice
(recipe page 16)

For dipping and accompaniments
soy sauce • shredded pickled ginger

Time *30 minutes + 45 minutes marinating time*
80 calories per piece

Nigiri Sushi with Anchovies

8 pieces • Particularly decorative

1 Wash the anchovies thoroughly and remove the heads. Remove the central bone but do not separate the fillets. Dry the fish with a cloth, sprinkle with salt, and leave it for 15 minutes. Rinse it under cold running water and dry with a cloth.

2 Peel and grate the ginger finely; mix with rice vinegar, mirin, and sugar until the sugar dissolves. Pour the marinade over the anchovies and steep them for 30 minutes. Dry them with a cloth and slash them across the skin at an angle, using a sharp knife.

3 Mix the wasabi powder with 3 tablespoons water and leave for a short while for the mixture to swell. Spread the underside of each anchovy with a little of the wasabi paste.

4 Form the sushi rice into eight cylindrical clumps and prepare Nigiri Sushi, using the anchovies and rice, as described on page 10.

5 Arrange the sushi pieces on a dish and serve with the remaining wasabi paste, soy sauce, and ginger. ■

Ingredients
4 oz oyster mushrooms
1 tbsp oil
1 tbsp soy sauce
1 tbsp mirin
2 oz firm tofu
1 scallion
2 tbsp wasabi powder
½ toasted nori sheet
acidulated water
⅔ cup prepared sushi rice
(recipe page 16)

For dipping and accompaniments
soy sauce • shredded pickled ginger

Time *30 minutes*
80 calories per piece

Nigiri Sushi with Oyster Mushrooms and Tofu

8 pieces • Sophisticated • Vegetarian

1 Clean the mushrooms and cut them into pieces. Heat the oil and sauté the mushrooms. Remove them from the heat and sprinkle them with the soy sauce and mirin. Leave to marinate for at least 30 minutes. Cut the tofu into eight sticks about 2 inches long. Clean and wash the scallions, and slice them into thin rings.

2 Combine the wasabi powder with 3 tablespoons water and leave it for

15 minutes to swell. Cut the sheet of toasted nori into eight strips, ½ inch wide.

3 Shape the rice into eight cylindrical clumps and spread with a little wasabi paste, using the fingertips. Garnish the rice with a piece of tofu and a few mushroom strips. Wrap each piece of sushi in a strip of nori. Secure the ends with a grain of rice. Sprinkle the prepared sushi with scallion rings and serve. ■

Nigiri Sushi
with Anchovies

Nigiri Sushi with Oyster
Mushrooms and Tofu

Ingredients

2 tsp peeled sesame seeds
4 fresh, fairly large shiitake
or field mushrooms
1 tbsp light soy sauce
¼ ripe avocado
a squeeze of lemon juice
2 tsp wasabi powder

For garnish

8 spring garlic stems
⅔ cup prepared sushi rice
(recipe page 16)

For dipping and accompaniments

soy sauce • wasabi paste
shredded pickled ginger

Time 35 minutes
80 calories per piece

Nigiri Sushi with Avocado and Mushrooms

8 pieces • Vegetarian

1 Toast the sesame seeds in a dry pan until golden brown. Remove and reserve.

2 Clean the mushrooms and cut them into thin slices. Heat the oil in a pan and sauté the mushrooms. Deglaze with soy sauce then remove from the heat and leave to cool.

3 Peel the avocado, cut the flesh first into slices and then into cubes. Sprinkle with lemon juice immediately to avoid discoloration.

4 Combine the wasabi paste with 3 tablespoons water to make a creamy paste and leave it to swell. Wash the garlic stems and pat them dry.

5 Make a little ball from 1 tablespoon of sushi rice, using wet hands. Flatten the balls slightly and spread the surface lightly with the wasabi paste.

6 Garnish the rice attractively with avocado cubes and mushroom slices. Sprinkle a few sesame seeds over the sushi pieces and decorate with the garlic stems. Arrange with pickled ginger and soy sauce for dipping. ■

Tip

Serve with finely grated radish, seasoned with a bit of wasabi paste, salt, and rice vinegar.

Variation

Use tender young zucchini instead of avocado.

Ingredients

For the omelet:
6 eggs
5 tbsp dashi (instant fish broth)
1 tsp light soy sauce
2 tbsp sugar
1 pinch of salt
1 tbsp mirin (Japanese cooking sherry)
oil for frying

Additionally:
1 toasted sheet of nori
⅔ cup prepared sushi rice (recipe page 16)

For dipping and accompaniments

soy sauce • wasabi paste
shredded pickled ginger

Time *50 minutes*
95 calories per piece

Nigiri Sushi with Omelet

8 pieces • Vegetarian

1 To make the omelet, beat the eggs and pour them into a bowl. Combine the cold dashi stock with the soy sauce, sugar, salt, and mirin until the sugar and salt dissolve. Add the mixture to the eggs. Beat with a whisk until combined, but do not beat it into a foam.

2 Pour the eggs into an oiled omelet pan and make an omelet ¾ inch thick, as described in the tip on this page.

3 Let the omelet cool to the room temperature. Slice it in half diagonally, then slice the halves into four even, rectangular pieces.

4 Cut the nori sheet into eight strips each ¾ inch wide. Shape the sushi rice into eight longish cylinders. Garnish each rice cylinder with a slice of omelet and press it down carefully. Wrap the Nigiri Sushi with a strip of nori around the middle. Secure the ends of the strips with a grain of rice. ■

Tip

The omelet will look best if cooked in a rectangular pan. You will find these pans in Japanese stores. A round pan will also do, but it should be at least 9½–10½ inches in diameter and have deep, straight sides. The Japanese use long cooking sticks for the preparation of the omelet, but less experienced cooks should use a flexible metal spatula to maneuver it in the pan.

Variation

Nigiri Sushi with Shrimp Omelet

Add the shrimp to the egg mixture. For this, marinate ½ cup shrimp in 4 tablespoons rice vinegar for one hour. Pour off the vinegar, mince the shrimp, and stir it into the egg mixture. Prepare the omelet as described in the recipe. Or use ½ cup of minced fish fillet instead of the shrimp.

Nippon's "kitchen-role" play

In terms of cuisine, they are fascinatingly sophisticated **morsels,** whose simple elegance is a **feast for the eyes.** Maki Sushi will waken the adventurer in you—all the varied and subtle fillings will simply leave you **craving for much more.**

Japan's "kitchen-roll"

An old Japanese proverb says that you get to live 75 days longer if you are lucky enough to eat something you have never eaten before.

You may find you are in luck with Maki Sushi, as it comes in countless varieties. Maki Sushi is always made with a sheet of nori, dried and pressed seaweed. Sticky rice containing a spicy filling is rolled into the nori sheet with the help of a flexible bamboo mat. The heart of the sushi roll, responsible for its flavor, may be fish, roe, seafood, omelet, vegetables, mushrooms, lettuce, and herbs. The sushi rolls are cut into handy pieces when ready. Since shapes and sizes vary, the individual bites are sometimes smaller, sometimes larger.

From Hoso- to Futo Maki

Sushi made from half a nori sheet is called Hoso-maki (thin sushi rolls). Those made from a whole nori sheet are called Futo Maki (thick sushi rolls). Ura Maki is an interesting variety of sushi that is turned "inside-out," whereby the sequence of rice and nori sheet has been reversed, so that the nori sheet is inside and the rice outside. Gunkan Maki (meaning "sushi in the shape of a battleship") has a soft filling inside. To prevent it slipping or dripping out, the rice clump is wrapped in a nori sheet in such a way that the strip of seaweed protrudes above the rice. This way, space is created for the filling and at the same time it is fenced in by the seaweed.

Just as you like it

There are no set rules with sushi as far as the eating order of the various sushi varieties is concerned. The only rule that applies here is pleasure. However, if you have prepared a selection of Maki Sushi and Nigiri Sushi, you should eat the Maki Sushi first, as the crisp nori sheets will soon become soggy and then tasteless if the moisture of the rice and filling penetrates them.

• To improve the visual appearance, when cutting the sushi rolls the second or third time, you can cut them diagonally.

Tips and Tricks for rolling and shaping

• If you don't have a bamboo mat for rolling you can use extra-strong aluminum foil. Dampen it well with vinegar water before use.
• It is especially important when preparing Maki Sushi to wet your palms and fingers with a vinegar-water mixture, otherwise the sticky rice will just stick to your fingers.
• The rice must be at room temperature. If it's too warm, the nori sheet will start to curl, while rice that is too cold doesn't stick together.
• Instead of using your hands, you can also spread the rice onto the nori sheet with a spoon. Before and in between spreading the rice, dip the spoon in the rice-vinegar water. Be careful not to crush the rice when spreading it.
• Beginners can spread the wasabi paste on the nori sheet rather than the rice. If children are going to eat as well, you can also leave out the hot green horseradish paste.
• If you are making sushi yourself more often, it is worthwhile to prepare larger quantities of spiced pumpkin or marinated shiitake mushrooms for fillings. You can store them in a screw-top jar for several weeks in the refrigerator.
• For Maki Sushi, you can make good use of leftovers from the preparation of Nigiri Sushi, such as pieces of fish fillet or omelet strips.

Multi-cultural-mix — for even more pleasure

The following recipes have mostly classic Japanese fillings. The California Roll (page 50) on the other hand, with its avocado and crabsticks or shrimp, is an American invention. A successful combination of cuisines and cultures brings much joy and pleasure when eating. Let your creativity guide you and don't hesitate to compose new fillings to match your tastes.

A little sushi quantity guide

As a snack or appetizer, one sushi roll, depending on thickness and fillings, can be cut into four to six pieces. Two pieces of Gunkan Maki constitute a serving. Depending on your appetite, for an entrée, you should calculate double or three times the amount unless you intend to serve other sushi varieties such as Nigiri or Temaki.

41

Ingredients
1 bunch chives
¼ ripe avocado
1 tsp lemon juice
4 oz fresh salmon fillet without the skin (the best wild or organic salmon)
2 toasted nori leaves
1¾ cups prepared sushi rice (recipe page 16)
1 tsp wasabi paste

For dipping and accompaniments
soy sauce • wasabi paste
shredded pickled ginger

Time *25 minutes*
65 calories per piece

Ingredients
8 small lettuce leaves
1 cucumber or pickle (about 4 in long)
10 oz fresh salmon fillet with skin (the best wild or organic salmon)
1 tbsp potato starch
3 tbsp oil
2 toasted nori leaves
1¾ cups prepared sushi rice (recipe page 16)
1 tsp wasabi paste

For dipping and accompaniments
soy sauce • wasabi paste
shredded pickled ginger

Time *35 minutes*
80 calories per piece

Hosomaki Sushi with Salmon and Avocado

24 pieces • Easy to make

1 Wash the chives and dry them with a cloth. Don't cut the stalks. Peel the avocado and cut it into eight strips. Sprinkle it with lemon juice immediately to avoid discoloration. Dry the salmon fillet with a cloth and cut it into ¼-inch wide strips. Cut the nori sheet diagonally in half.

2 Make Maki Sushi (see page 11) using the prepared ingredients, the rice, and wasabi paste. Cut the four sushi rolls into six equal pieces and arrange them decoratively on a plate, cut side upward. ■

Hosomaki Sushi with Crisp Salmon

16 pieces • Sophisticated

1 Wash and dry the lettuce and the cucumber. Peel the cucumber or pickle leaving it whole, then cut into long strips ¼ inch thick and ¼ inch wide.

2 Pat the salmon dry and sprinkle with potato starch. Heat the oil in a frying pan and sauté the salmon, skin side down over high heat for two minutes or until crisp. Turn and sauté for another minute. Remove from the pan and drain on kitchen paper. Slice the salmon into strips and slice the nori sheet in two diagonally.

3 Make Maki Sushi (see page 11) from the prepared ingredients, the rice, and wasabi paste, using a rolling mat. Arrange the ingredients along the narrow side of the nori sheet and let the lettuce and cucumber protrude a little beyond the nori at each end. Cut each sushi roll into four pieces each. ■

Hosomaki Sushi
with Crisp Salmon

Hosomaki Sushi with
Salmon and Avocado

Ingredients

1 scallion or 2 baby leeks
4 oz fresh tuna fillet
2 toasted nori sheets
1¾ cups prepared sushi rice
(recipe page 16)
1 tsp wasabi paste

For dipping and accompaniments
soy sauce • wasabi paste
shredded pickled ginger

Time *30 minutes*
30 calories per piece

Hosomaki Sushi with Ground Tuna

24 pieces • Easy to prepare

1 Wash, clean, dry, and chop the scallions or leeks. Dry the tuna fillet with a cloth and dice it. Mince the scallions or leeks with the diced tuna on a plastic chopping board, using a sharp knife. Cut the nori sheets diagonally in half.

2 Make Maki Sushi (see page 11) using the prepared ingredients, rice, and wasabi paste. Slice the four sushi rolls into six equal-sized pieces. Arrange them decoratively on a serving platter with the cut side facing upward. ■

Ingredients

4 oz very fresh tuna fillet
2 tsp low-fat mayonnaise
1 tsp sesame oil
1 tsp rice vinegar
¼ tsp shichimi togarashi
(hot spice mixture)
2 toasted nori sheets
1¾ cups prepared sushi rice
(recipe page 16)

To garnish
shichimi togarashi • finely
chopped scallions or chives

For dipping and accompaniments
soy sauce • wasabi paste
shredded pickled ginger

Time *30 minutes*
30 calories per piece

Hosomaki Sushi with Marinated Tuna

24 pieces • Spicy

1 Dry the fish fillet with a cloth and cut into ½-inch wide strips. Combine the mayonnaise, sesame oil, rice vinegar, and the blend of spices in a shallow bowl. Dip the tuna strips into the mixture. Cover it and leave them in it for five minutes to marinate. In the meantime, cut the nori sheets diagonally in half.

2 Make Maki Sushi (see page 11) from the tuna and rice. Cut the four sushi rolls into six even pieces. Arrange with the cut side upward. Season to taste with the spices and garnish with finely chopped scallions or chives. ■

Hosomaki Sushi with
Marinated Tuna

Hosomaki Sushi with
Ground Tuna

Ingredients

1 large carrot
*1 4-in piece cucumber or
zucchini*
3 tbsp sake
½ tsp sugar
¼ tsp salt
2 toasted nori sheets
*1¾ cups prepared sushi rice
(recipe page 12)*
1 tsp wasabi paste

For dipping and accompaniments
*soy sauce • wasabi paste
shredded pickled ginger*

Time *30 minutes
25 calories per piece*

Hosomaki Sushi with Carrot and Cucumber

24 pieces • Simple

1 Peel the carrots and slice them lengthwise into strips ⅛ inch thick, then into slices ⅛ inch long. Wash the cucumber or zucchini and pat dry. Cut off ⅛-inch thick strips without peeling. Then slice into batons ⅛ inch thick.

2 In a pan, bring the sake, 2 tablespoons water, sugar, and salt to the boil. Add the carrot strips and simmer, uncovered, for 1 minute. Remove from the heat, add the cucumber or zucchini strips to the carrots and leave the vegetables to cool in the water. Remove them and pat them dry on kitchen paper.

3 Halve the nori sheets diagonally. Make the Maki Sushi from the prepared ingredients, the sushi rice, and the wasabi paste, with the help of a rolling mat (see page 11). Slice each of the four sushi rolls into six pieces, and serve. ■

Ingredients

½ cup raw pumpkin flesh
1 tsp salt
*⅔ cup dashi (instant fish
broth) or water*
2 tsp sugar
2 tbsp soy sauce
1 tbsp mirin (Japanese cooking sherry) or rice wine
2 toasted nori sheets
*1¾ cups prepared sushi rice
(recipe page 16)*

For dipping and accompaniments
*soy sauce • wasabi paste
shredded pickled ginger*

Time *30 minutes
25 calories per piece*

Hosomaki Sushi with Pumpkin

16 pieces • Sophisticated

1 Rinse the pumpkin briefly. Sprinkle your hands with the salt and rub it into the pumpkin flesh. Leave for 5 minutes. Rinse and drain the pumpkin and place it in a saucepan. Cover with water and bring to the boil. Cook for 10 minutes then drain it.

2 Pour the dashi or water into another pan and add the pumpkin. Add the sugar, soy sauce, and mirin. Simmer on low heat, uncovered, until most of the liquid has evaporated. Leave the pumpkin to cool and pat it dry.

3 Slice each sheet of nori crosswise into two halves. Make Maki Sushi, using strips of the prepared pumpkin and the sushi rice, with the help of a rolling mat (see page 11). Slice each sushi roll into four equal-sized pieces. ■

Hosomaki Sushi with Carrot and Cucumber

Hosomaki Sushi with Pumpkin

Hosomaki Sushi with Shiitake Mushrooms

16 pieces • Sophisticated

Ingredients
*4 large dried shiitake
mushrooms
1 tbsp sugar
3 tbsp soy sauce
2 tbsp mirin (Japanese
cooking sherry)
1 scallion
2 toasted nori sheets
1¾ cups prepared sushi rice
(recipe page 16)
1 tsp wasabi paste*

For dipping and accompaniments
*soy sauce • wasabi paste
shredded pickled ginger*

Time *30 minutes (+ 20 minutes soaking time)
35 calories per piece*

1 Pour ⅔ cup of boiling water over the mushrooms and let it soak for 20 minutes. Strain through a fine sieve, collecting the soaking water in a bowl. Rinse the mushrooms thoroughly and remove the tough stems.

2 Bring the mushroom soaking water, sugar, soy sauce, and mirin to the boil. Simmer the mushrooms for ten minutes, stirring occasionally. Drain them into a sieve. Slice the mushroom caps into strips.

3 Wash, clean, and dry the scallions and slice them into thin rings. Halve the nori sheets diagonally. Make Maki Sushi (see page 11) from the prepared ingredients, the rice, and wasabi paste, using a rolling mat.
Cut the four sushi rolls in six pieces equal in size. Arrange with the cut side facing upward. ■

Hosomaki Sushi with Cucumber and Sesame

16 pieces • Easy to prepare

Ingredients
*4 tsp sesame seeds
1 cucumber (about 4 in
long)
2 toasted nori sheets
1¾ cups prepared sushi rice
(recipe page 16)
1 tsp wasabi paste*

For dipping and accompaniments
*soy sauce • wasabi paste
shredded pickled ginger*

Time *25 minutes
20 calories per piece*

1 Toast the sesame seeds in a small dry pan until golden brown. Remove from the pan and set aside to cool.

2 Wash and dry the cucumber. Peel it with a long knife, then slice it into long strips around ¼ inch thick and ¼ inch wide.

3 Halve the nori sheet diagonally. Make Maki Sushi (see page 11) from the prepared ingredients, the rice, and wasabi paste, using a rolling mat. Cut the four sushi rolls in six equal-sized pieces. Arrange with the cut side facing upward. ■

**Hosomaki Sushi with
Cucumber and Sesame**

**osomaki Sushi with
hiitake Mushrooms**

Ingredients
3 tbsp sesame seeds
4 crabsticks (around 2 oz)
1 cucumber (about 4 in long)
¼ ripe avocado
1 tsp lemon juice
2 toasted nori sheets
1 cup prepared sushi rice
(recipe page 16)
1 tbsp low-fat mayonnaise

For dipping and accompaniments
soy sauce • wasabi paste
shredded pickled ginger

Time *30 minutes*
20 calories per piece

Ura Maki Sushi: California Roll

24 pieces • Great for entertaining

1 Toast the sesame seeds in a small dry pan until golden brown. Remove them and leave them to cool.

2 Dry the crabsticks and halve them lengthwise. Wash and dry the cucumber. Peel it with a long knife and slice it into strips around ¼ inch thick and ¼ inch wide. Peel the avocado quarter and cut it into strips. Sprinkle it with lemon juice immediately to avoid discoloration. Cover a bamboo mat with clingfilm. Place a nori sheet on it, smooth side downward. With wet hands, arrange half of the sushi rice on the nori sheet leaving a margin along the longer edges, i.e. top and bottom. Turn the sheet carefully, so that the rice is now underneath and the nori sheet is on top (see page 12).

3 Squirt or spread a thin line of mayonnaise on the lower third of the nori sheet and place half of the crabsticks, cucumber, and avocado strips on it. Roll up the rice, nori sheet, and the filling using a rolling mat. Make another roll with the remaining ingredients in the same way.

4 Slice the sushi rolls into six even-sized pieces respectively. Dip one end of each piece in the toasted sesame seeds. ∎

Variation
Ura Maki Sushi with Salmon
For the filling: wash a large carrot and slice it into finger thick strips and blanch them. Blanch 1 cup leaf spinach in salted water, refresh in cold water, and drain thoroughly. Slice 4 ounces very fresh salmon fillet into finger-thick strips and marinate in a small quantity of mirin. Prepare as described in the recipe.

Ingredients

4 large dried shiitake mushrooms
1 tbsp sugar
3 tbsp soy sauce
4 tbsp mirin (Japanese cooking sherry)
salt
1 cup leaf spinach
4 cooked, shelled bay shrimp
1 cucumber (about 4 in long)
4 strips prepared dried pumpkin (see instructions page 46)
3 oz omelet (see instructions page 36 and the Tip on the same page)
3 toasted nori sheets
1 cup prepared sushi rice (recipe page 16)

For dipping and accompaniments
soy sauce • wasabi paste
shredded pickled ginger

Time *50 minutes (+ 20 minutes soaking time)*
For 12 pieces, 50 calories per piece

Futo Maki with Bay Shrimp, Omelet, and Mushrooms

8–12 pieces • Allow plenty of time for preparation

1 Soak the dried mushrooms in ⅔ cup hot water for 20 minutes. Strain through a fine sieve and collect the soaking water in a bowl. Rinse the mushrooms thoroughly and remove the tough stems.

2 Pour the soaking water from the mushrooms into a pan and add the sugar, soy sauce, and 2 tablespoons mirin. Bring to the boil. Add the mushrooms and simmer for 10 minutes. Strain through a sieve.

3 While the mushrooms are cooking, bring some salted water to the boil. Wash and clean the spinach and cook it in the boiling water for 30 seconds. Drain it in a sieve, refresh in ice-cold water, and drain again. Squeeze the spinach to remove excess moisture. Slice the shrimp in half lengthwise and dip them in the rest of the mirin. Wash, drain and peel the cucumber. Slice it lengthwise in strips ½ inch thick, using a long knife. Cut it into strips around ½ inch wide. Cut the cooked shiitake mushrooms into strips, as well. Dry the prepared pumpkin strips with a cloth and slice the prepared omelet lengthwise into ½-inch wide strips.

4 Prepare large Maki Sushi using a rolling mat (see page 11). In order to do so, put a whole nori sheet on a rolling mat. Wet your hands and place half of the prepared sushi rice on it, leaving a margin at the sides. Halve another nori sheet diagonally and arrange the rice on it in such a way that it seals the bottom edge of the other nori sheet. Press it down a little and put half of the prepared ingredients on top. Shape the ingredients into a thick roll. Make another roll from the remaining ingredients. Cut the two sushi rolls into four to six pieces. ∎

Tip

This type of sushi goes well with Nigiri Sushi with Omelet (page 36). If you do so, you can make an omelet with less egg. Instead of cucumber, you could also use ½ inch thick blanched carrot batons.

Ingredients
2 nori leaves
2 eggs
2 tsp sugar
1 pinch of salt
2 tbsp oil
1 handful spinach leaves
(around ¾ cup)
2 tsp wasabi powder
3 oz smoked salmon
3 tbsp feta cheese
1¾ cups prepared sushi rice
(recipe page 16)

For dipping and accompaniments
shredded pickled ginger

Time: *40 minutes*
80 calories per piece

Futo Maki with Smoked Salmon

16 pieces • Sophisticated

1 Toast the nori sheet on one side, one after another in a small dry nonstick pan without fat on medium heat until they become fragrant. Remove and reserve them.

2 Beat the eggs with sugar and a dash of salt. Heat the oil in a pan, pour the egg mixture into it, and make a set omelet.

3 Wash the spinach and blanch it in boiling salted water for 30 seconds. Refresh in cold water and let it drain thoroughly on kitchen towel.

4 Stir the wasabi powder with 3 table-spoons water into a creamy paste and let it swell. Slice the omelet and the salmon into strips. Crumble the feta cheese.

5 Form Maki Sushi (page 11) from the prepared ingredients, using a bamboo rolling mat. Leave the nori sheet uncut and spread double amount of rice over the surface.

6 First, halve the rolls and then cut the halves into four equal pieces. ■

Variation
In the asparagus season, instead of spinach for the filling make use of lightly cooked green asparagus, marinated briefly in soy sauce and rice vinegar.

Futo Maki with Smoked Trout

16 pieces • Easy to make • Sophisticated

Ingredients
4 oz white radish
4 oz smoked trout fillet
3 cups spinach
salt
2 tsp wasabi powder
2 toasted nori sheets
acidulated water
1¾ cups prepared sushi rice
(recipe page 16)

For dipping and accompaniments
soy sauce • wasabi paste
shredded pickled ginger

Time *40 minutes*
45 calories per piece

1 Clean and wash the radish and slice it lengthwise into strips. Do the same with the trout fillet, using a sharp knife.

2 Trim the spinach, wash it, and blanch in boiling salted water for 3 minutes. Remove it, refresh in cold water, and squeeze out excess moisture. Place the spinach on kitchen towels and loosen again a little.

3 Stir the wasabi powder with 3 tablespoons water and leave to swell.

4 Make a thick Futo Maki roll (see page 11) from half of the prepared ingredients and a whole nori sheet, using a bamboo rolling mat.

5 Rinse a sharp knife in acidulated water and use it to slice half the rolls diagonally with it. Slice both halves into four equal-sized pieces. ■

Gunkan Maki with Trout Roe

8 pieces • A classic • Quick to make

Ingredients
2 toasted nori sheets
1 lime
2 tsp wasabi powder
acidulated water
1 cup prepared sushi rice
(recipe page 16)
uncooked rice grains
3 oz trout roe
1 piece of cucumber
(about 1 in long)

For dipping and accompaniments
soy sauce • wasabi paste
shredded pickled ginger

Time *20 minutes*
75 calories per piece

1 Cut each nori sheet into four strips, approximately 6 inches long and 1¼ inch wide.

2 Wash the lime in hot water, dry it, and cut four paper-thin slices from the middle and quarter them. Squeeze the juice from the remaining lime halves. Stir 3 tablespoons of the juice with the wasabi powder and let it swell for a short while.

3 Moisten your hands with acidulated water and shape oval clumps from the sushi rice. Wrap a nori strip around each clump, leaving a protruding edge; the smooth side should face outward. Secure the end of each strip with a rice grain.

4 Press the rice down slightly, spread a little of the wasabi over it, and fill with roe.

5 Wash the cucumber, half it removing the seeds, and slice it finely. Stick a few cucumber slices and a piece of lime in a fan-shape into the roe. ■

Gunkan Maki
with Trout Roe

Futo Maki with
Smoked Trout

Ingredients
¾ cup shrimp
1 tbsp low-fat mayonnaise
2 tsp mirin (Japanese
cooking sherry)
2 tsp lemon juice
2 bunches chives
2 toasted nori sheets
1 cup prepared sushi rice
(recipe page 16)
1 tsp wasabi paste

For dipping and accompaniments
soy sauce • wasabi paste
shredded pickled ginger

Time 20 minutes
65 calories per piece

Gunkan Maki with Shrimp

8 pieces • For special occasions

1 Dry the shrimp with a cloth and chop them coarsely. Combine the mayonnaise, mirin, and lemon juice and mix with the shrimp. Wash and drain the chives and slice them into 2½-3-inch sections. Trim the ragged edges of the nori sheets and cut them alongside into eight strips approximately 1 inch wide and 6 inches long.

2 Wet your hands and make eight oval clumps from the sushi rice. Wrap a nori sheet, with the smooth side facing out-ward, around each clump of rice (see page 12). Secure the end of the sheet with one or two rice grains.

3 Press the rice in the nori sheet down carefully. Spread three-quarters of the shrimp mixture evenly over the rice. Arrange six to seven sections of chive on top. Add the remaining shrimp. Form eight small balls from the wasabi paste and garnish the sushi with them. ∎

Ingredients
2 toasted nori sheets
1 cup prepared sushi rice
(recipe page 16)
6 tbsp salmon or trout roe
4 peeled cucumbers, cut into
thin slices
1 tsp wasabi paste

For dipping and accompaniments
soy sauce • wasabi paste
shredded pickled ginger

Time 20 minutes
45 calories per piece

Gunkan Maki with Salmon Roe

8 pieces • A classic

1 Trim the ragged edges of the nori sheets with a knife and slice the nori sheets lengthwise into eight strips about 1 inch wide and 6 inches long.

2 Wet your hands and make eight oval clumps from the sushi rice. Wrap a nori sheet with the smooth side facing out-ward around each clump of rice (see page 12). Secure the ends with one or two rice grains.

3 Press down the rice carefully and spread the roe evenly over it.

4 Halve the cucumber slices and cut them into a fan shape, leaving them unpeeled. Insert this as decoration between the rice and the roe. Shape eight small balls from the wasabi paste and garnish the sushi with it. ∎

Gunkan Maki
with Salmon Roe

Gunkan Maki
with Shrimp

Sushi cones in a trice

Temaki represents another sushi variation, this time in the shape of a **bag or tiny sack.** For the fillings **cooked meat and chicken** are used, delicately flavored with **spicy sauces.** Both adults and children enjoy sushi served this way.

Pure pleasure—bite after bite

Not all sushi varieties are elaborate and expensive. Temaki Sushi, for instance, is a commoner version of Maki Sushi that can be prepared quickly and with little effort, and tastes just as great with inexpensive ingredients. Hand-rolled Temaki represent the modern aspect of the sushi repertoire. A piece of nori is put into the left palm and covered with sticky rice; then filling is placed on top of it before being rolled up into a cone shape. Sushi experts manage to do it effortlessly with just one hand, the left hand. Beginners will probably need help from their right hand at first. When eating, just take the cone in your hand, dip the top in the soy sauce and bite it off. Dip in the sauce again before each bite.

Fillings without end

You can fill Temaki Sushi with anything you like. Fish and seafood, fish roe, meat, chicken, vegetables, mushrooms, herbs, and sprouts, all can be varied and complement one another according to taste. Marinades for fish and meat as well as spicy sauces add even more flavor to the equation. And by the way, all the fillings used in preparation for Maki Sushi can also be used in Temaki Sushi.

Instead of nori sheets try using lettuce leaves

As a witty variation or in case you run out of nori sheets, wrap the filling in lettuce leaves. Flawless iceberg, oakleaf, or romaine lettuce leaves as well as lollo rosso and lollo biondo are especially recommended for this purpose. However you will have to wrap the "lettuce cones" tightly in the bottom third so that the filling won't fall out. For a "ribbon" you can use narrow strips of spiced pumpkin (recipe page 12), nori sheets, blanched carrots, or leeks. It is better to tie the ends of the strips into a knot—this is not only practical but also looks very attractive. Serve the sushi as soon as possible after making it.

Tips & Tricks for Temaki Sushi

• If you can't get hold of toasted nori sheets, you can toast them yourself: simply hold them carefully over a gas flame or toast over medium heat in a dry pan until fragrant. The sheets will become dark green and crisp in the process.

• a seaweed snack: toast any remaining nori sheets as described above in a pan, break into small pieces, and eat while still warm.

• If you want to fill Temaki Sushi with semi-liquid or soft ingredients, fill the bottom part of the nori cone with sushi rice before you start adding the other ingredients

• Fresh daikon sprouts are a common ingredient for Temaki Sushi and Maki Sushi in Japan. You may be lucky enough to find them in an oriental grocery store. You can also grow radish sprouts yourself from Japanese radish seeds (giant summer radish) in a planter or window-box. Their spicy, peppery flavor, similar to that of watercress, goes well with all types of sushi, including those made with omelets, among others.

• Shiso leaves, sold in plastic bags, are also sometimes available. They are mostly used in combination with white meat but are also a suitable alternative to lettuce leaves in Temaki Sushi with Crabsticks and Avocado (page 66).

• Small pieces of Temaki Sushi are an ideal appetizer or finger food for buffets and parties.

Invitation to a Sushi Party

Temaki Sushi is so popular in Japan that many bars offer a selection of ingredients from which you can choose to fill the Temaki yourself. This is also a great idea for using at home. Invite your guests to a sushi party. Place all the fixings on a large table or sideboard. You will need plenty of nori sheets and lettuce leaves, sushi rice, and a selection of ingredients for all kinds of fillings. Don't forget to serve wasabi paste, soy sauce, and pickled ginger for dipping.

It is also important to provide small finger-bowls containing acidulated water for hand-wetting. Any of the ingredients mentioned in this book are suitable as fillings. Each guest can create their own individual filling. A piece of such made with half a nori sheet will be around the size of an ice-cream cone. If you use a quarter of a nori sheet you will make them smaller. This has the advantage of enabling you to try out more of the various ingredients.

Ingredients
1 piece white radish (4 oz)
1 small dried red chili
pepper
6 oz fresh tuna fillet
2 tbsp soy sauce
2 tbsp mirin (Japanese
cooking sherry)
1 tsp lemon juice
2 toasted nori sheets
1 cup prepared sushi rice
(recipe page 16)
1 tsp wasabi paste

For dipping and accompaniments
soy sauce • wasabi paste
shredded pickled ginger

Time 20 minutes
150 calories per piece

Temaki Sushi with Tuna, Chili Pepper, and Radish

4 pieces • Spicy

1 Peel the radish and carve a whole in the middle of the cut with a knife. Put the chili inside it and grate the radish finely together with the chili.

2 Pat the tuna dry with a cloth or kitchen paper and cut it into strips less than ½ inch wide. Stir the soy sauce with the mirin and lemon juice. Dip fish strips in it. Squeeze out the chili radish. Halfe the nori sheets diagonally. Wet your

hands and shape the sushi rice into four little, equal-sized balls.

3 Form cone-like Temaki Sushi from the nori sheets with rice, wasabi paste and the prepared ingredients (see page 13). ■

Ingredients
2 small scallions
6 oz fresh tuna fillet
2 toasted nori sheets
1 cup prepared sushi rice
(recipe page 16)
1 tsp wasabi paste

For dipping and accompaniments
soy sauce • wasabi paste
shredded pickled ginger

Time 20 minutes
140 calories per piece

Temaki Sushi with Ground Tuna

4 pieces • Easy to prepare

1 Wash and clean the scallions, shake off the water, and cut into sections. Dry the tuna fillet with a cloth and dice it. Chop the onions and mix with the tuna on a kitchen chopping board.

2 Halve the nori sheets diagonally. Wet your hands and shape four small balls

from the sushi rice. Then make cones from the nori sheets into which you insert the rice, wasabi paste, and the prepared ingredients for making cone-like Temaki Sushi (see page 13).

3 Arrange the Temaki decoratively and serve immediately. ■

Temaki Sushi
with Ground Tuna

Temaki Sushi with Tuna,
Chili Pepper, and Radish

Ingredients

4 small lettuce leaves
1 small shallot
¼ ripe avocado
1 tsp lemon juice
4 crabsticks
2 toasted nori sheets
1 cup prepared sushi rice
(recipe page 16)
1 tsp wasabi paste

For dipping and accompaniments
soy sauce • wasabi paste
shredded pickled ginger

Time *20 minutes*
65 calories per piece

Temaki Sushi with Crabsticks and Avocado

4 pieces • A favorite with kids

1 Wash and drain the lettuce. Peel the shallots and slice them lengthwise into thin strips. Rinse briefly in water and dry with a cloth. Peel the avocado and slice it lengthwise into four strips. Sprinkle the strips with lemon juice to prevent discoloration.

2 Dry the crabsticks with a cloth.

3 Halve the nori sheets diagonally. With wet hands, shape the sushi rice into four small balls.

4 Shape the nori sheets into Temaki Sushi cones. Fill with the rice, wasabi paste, and the prepared ingredients (see page 13). ∎

Ingredients

1 piece white radish (about 2 oz)
1 cucumber (about 4 in long)
6 oz fresh salmon fillet with skin
½ tbsp potato starch
2 tbsp oil
2 toasted nori sheets
1 cup prepared sushi rice
(recipe page 16)
1 tsp wasabi paste

For dipping and accompaniments
soy sauce • wasabi paste
shredded pickled ginger

Time *25 minutes*
175 calories per piece

Temaki Sushi with Salmon and Cucumber

4 pieces • Sophisticated

1 Peel the radish and first cut it into paper-thin slices, then into narrow strips. Wash the cucumber, slice it lengthwise into strips about ½ inch thick and slice the strips into batons, discarding the seeds.

2 Dry the salmon fillet with a cloth and dust it with potato starch. Fry in a nonstick pan in hot oil on each side for 1–2 minutes. Drain the salmon on kitch- en paper and cut it into slices around ½-inch thick slices. Rinse the radish briefly in water and squeeze it out. Halve the nori sheets diagonally. Wet your hands and shape the sushi rice into four balls.

3 Shape the nori sheets into cones to make Temaki Sushi. Add the rice, wasabi paste, and the prepared ingredients (see page 13). ∎

Temaki Sushi with
Crabsticks and Avocado

Temaki Sushi
with Salmon
and Cucumber

Ingredients
*1 cup mixed mushrooms
(such as shiitake, oyster
mushrooms, ceps, and
portobello mushrooms)
4 small scallions
1 tbsp butter
1 tbsp oil
1 tsp soy sauce
1 pinch of salt
pepper
1 tsp lemon juice
2 toasted nori sheets
1 cup prepared sushi rice
(recipe page 16)
1 tsp wasabi paste*

For dipping and accompaniments
*soy sauce • wasabi paste
shredded pickled ginger*

Time *25 minutes
105 calories per piece*

Temaki Sushi with Mixed Mushrooms
4 pieces • Vegetarian • A favorite with kids

1 Rub the mushrooms with a kitchen cloth and lightly brush the gills. If necessary, wash the mushrooms briefly and let them dry on kitchen paper. Slice the mushrooms, discarding any tough stems or damaged parts. Wash and clean the scallions and slice the green parts into sections approximately 2 inches long. Slice these into thin strips. Dry them with a cloth.

2 Heat the butter and oil in a large pan. Sauté the mushrooms over medium heat, stirring frequently, until all the moisture has evaporated. Add the soy sauce and season with salt, pepper, and lemon juice.

3 Halve the nori sheets diagonally using scissors. Wet your hands and shape the sushi rice into four equal-sized balls.

4 Make cones from the nori sheets for Temaki Sushi. Fill them with the rice, wasabi paste, scallion sections, and the cooked mushrooms (see page 13). ■

Tip
Using lettuce or other salad leaves instead of nori sheets will make the Temaki Sushi even more attractive. You must use absolutely unblemished lettuce leaves. You can use butterhead lettuce, lollo rosso, iceberg lettuce, or red oakleaf lettuce, or even Belgian endive. To make sure that the "cones" keep their shape you can tie them with strips of scallion or marinated pumpkin and knot the ends.

Ingredients

4 green asparagus stalks
salt • 1 tbsp rice vinegar
1 tbsp mirin
14 oz oyster mushrooms
2 tbsp oil • pepper
1 tbsp soy sauce
1 tbsp lemon juice
1 tsp wasabi powder
2 scallions
4 toasted nori sheets
acidulated water
1¾ cups prepared sushi rice
(recipe page 16)
uncooked rice grains

For dipping and accompaniments
soy sauce • shredded pickled
ginger

Time 30 minutes
100 calories per piece

Ingredients

1 tsp wasabi powder • ½ ripe
avocado • 1 tbsp lemon
juice • 1 small zucchini
10 oz fresh salmon fillet
4 toasted nori sheets
acidulated water
1¾ cups prepared sushi rice
(recipe page 16)
uncooked rice grains
4 tbsp salmon roe

For dipping and accompaniments
soy sauce • shredded pickled
ginger

Time 30 minutes
175 calories per piece

Temaki Sushi with Asparagus and Mushrooms

8 pieces • Particularly decorative • Vegetarian

1 Wash the asparagus stems, trim the ends, and peel the lower half. Halve lengthwise. Blanch the asparagus for approximately one minute, refresh in cold water, dry with a cloth, and sprinkle with rice vinegar and mirin.

2 Clean the mushrooms and slice them into strips. Heat the oil and fry the mushrooms in it stirring from time to time until the moisture evaporates. Season them to taste with salt, pepper, soy sauce, and lemon juice.

3 Stir the wasabi powder with 3 tablespoons water and leave it to swell. Clean, wash, and slice the scallions lengthwise into strips approximately 2 inches long.

4 Halve the nori sheets diagonally. Wet you hands and shape the sushi rice into four small balls.

5 Make Temaki Sushi cones from the nori sheets and fill with rice, wasabi paste, and the prepared ingredients (see page 13). ■

Temaki Sushi with Salmon and Avocado

8 pieces • Particularly decorative • Vegetarian

1 Stir the wasabi powder with 3 tablespoons of water and let it swell for a short while.

2 Peel the avocado half, cut the pulp lengthwise into eight strips, and brush with lemon juice. Clean the zucchini, wash it, and slice it lengthwise into sticks. Dry the salmon fillet with a cloth and cut it lengthwise in finger- thick strips.

3 Halve the nori sheets diagonally. Wet your hands with acidulated water and shape the sushi rice into eight balls.

4 Shape the nori sheets into cones for Temaki Sushi and fill them with rice, wasabi paste, and the prepared ingredients (see page 13). Spread some salmon roe on each cone and serve. ■

Temaki Sushi with Asparagus and Mushrooms

Temaki Sushi with Salmon and Avocado

Ingredients

For the pumpkin:
4 dried pumpkin strips
1 tsp salt
1 tsp sugar
1½ tbsp soy sauce
1 tbsp mirin (Japanese cooking sherry)

For the omelet:
4 eggs
4 tbsp dashi (instant fish broth)
½ tsp light soy sauce
1 tbsp sugar
2 tsp mirin (Japanese cooking sherry)
1 dash salt
oil for frying

Additionally:
2 oz cucumber
2 toasted nori sheets
1 cup prepared sushi rice (recipe page 16)

For dipping and accompaniments
soy sauce • wasabi paste
shredded pickled ginger

Time *50 minutes (+ 20 minutes soaking time)*
180 calories per piece

Temaki Sushi with Omelet, Cucumber, and Pumpkin

4 pieces • A little more time-consuming • Vegetarian

1 Rinse the pumpkin strips briefly in water. Rub them in your palms with salt to soften them slightly and rinse again. Soak the pumpkin in warm water for at least 20 minutes.

2 In the meantime, crack the eggs for the omelet into a bowl. In another bowl, combine the dashi, soy sauce, sugar, mirin. Whisk well together and add to the eggs. Whisk with an egg-beater but don't beat until frothy. Make a ¾-inch thick omelet from the egg dough in a small pan, if possible a rectangular Japanese one. Remove it from the pan and leave it to cool.

3 Meanwhile, drain the pumpkin strips, cover with fresh water, bring to the boil, simmer for 10 minutes, and drain again.

4 Cover the pumpkin with fresh water. Add sugar, soy sauce, and mirin. Simmer, uncovered, on medium heat until almost all the liquid has evaporated.

5 Wash the cucumber and dry it with a cloth. Cut it into strips just under ½ inch thick and halve these diagonally. Slice the nori sheets diagonally in half with scissors. Let the pumpkin cool and dry it with a cloth. Halve the cold omelet diagonally and cut it into eight equal strips. Wet your hands and shape the sushi rice into four balls.

6 Shape the nori sheets into cones for Temaki Sushi and fill them with rice, wasabi paste, omelet, pumpkin, and cucumber strips (see page 13). Arrange the Temaki Sushi on a plate. ■

Ingredients

For the sesame sauce:
1 tbsp dashi (instant fish broth) or water
½ tbsp sugar
1 tbsp light soy sauce
1 tbsp mirin (Japanese cooking sherry)
2 tbsp sesame paste (in a jar)

Additionally:
2 tbsp sesame seeds
4 oz chicken breast fillet
1 x ½in piece of fresh ginger
2–3 medium white cabbage leaves
salt
½ cup spinach leaves
2 toasted nori sheets
1 cup prepared sushi rice (recipe page 16)

For dipping and accompaniments

soy sauce • wasabi paste
shredded pickled ginger

Time *45 minutes*
80 calories per piece

Temaki Sushi with Chicken Breast

8 pieces • Spicy • Sophisticated

1 For the sesame sauce: add the dashi or water with the sugar until it has dissolved. Add soy sauce, mirin, and sesame paste and stir until smooth.

2 Toast the sesame seeds on medium heat until golden-brown in a small dry pan, stirring frequently. Remove from the pan and put aside.

3 Put the chicken breast fillet into a pot and cover with water. Peel the ginger, halve it, and add it to the pot. Bring it to the boil and simmer gently on medium heat for three minutes.

4 In the meantime, wash and clean the white cabbage. Slice the leaves into small rectangles. Add the cabbage and 1–2 dashes of salt to the chicken. Simmer for further 5–7 minutes or until the cabbage softens.

5 Meanwhile, bring salted water to the boil. Wash, clean, and blanch the spinach in the boiling water for 30 seconds. Refresh in ice-cold water and drain it. Squeeze it thoroughly and spread it out to dry.

6 Transfer the chicken breast and cabbage to a sieve, refresh in ice-cold water, and drain. Remove the ginger. Dice the meat into bite-sized pieces and stir thoroughly with the cabbage and sesame sauce.

7 Cut the nori sheets in four. Wet your hands and shape the sushi rice into eight balls. Shape the nori sheets into cones for Temaki Sushi and fill them with the rice, spinach, and the chicken-and-cabbage mixture (see page 13). Sprinkle sesame seeds over the filling. ■

Variation

Temaki Sushi with pork

Cook 3½ ounces lean pork in the same way as the chicken. Instead of white cabbage, slice a carrot into fine strips. Add to the meat and cook until al dente. Prepare the Temaki Sushi as described in the recipe.

Ingredients

*For the garlic and
ginger sauce:*
*2 tbsp dashi (instant fish
broth)*
3 tbsp soy sauce
*2 tbsp mirin (Japanese
cooking sherry)*
½ garlic clove
1 x ½-in piece fresh ginger
*1 small piece kombu sea-
weed*

Additionally:
1 tbsp sesame seeds
*8 small iceberg lettuce
leaves*
1 bunch chives
½ carrot
*1 small piece white radish
(2 oz)*
6 oz lean beef
salt
pepper
2 tbsp oil
½ toasted nori sheet
*1 cup prepared sushi rice
(recipe page 16)*
1 thin slice untreated lemon

For dipping and accompaniments
*soy sauce • wasabi paste
shredded pickled ginger*

Time *45 minutes (+ resting
time overnight)*
170 calories per piece

Temaki Sushi with Beef Strips
4 pieces • For special occasions • Particularly ornamental

1 Prepare the garlic and ginger sauce the night before, stirring the dashi with soy sauce and mirin. Peel the garlic and ginger and squeeze both through a garlic press into the sauce. Add the kombu and let the sauce rest, covered, overnight.

2 Remove the kombu from the sauce the following day. Toast the sesame seeds in a small, dry pan on medium heat until golden brown, stirring frequently. Remove from the pan and reserve.

3 Wash and clean the lettuce leaves. Drain them well and pat them dry with a cloth. Peel the carrots and the radish. Slice both lengthwise into thin slices, then into very fine strips. Rinse the radish briefly with cold water, drain it, and pat it dry.

4 Dry the beef fillet with a cloth, and season it on both sides with salt and pepper. Heat the oil in a frying pan and sauté the meat on each side over medium to high heat for 2–4 minutes. Remove and drain on kitchen paper. Slice the fillet against the grain in very thin slices. Dip them in the garlic and ginger and soy sauce.

5 Cut half the nori sheet with scissors into four narrow strips. Wet your hands and shape four balls from the sushi rice.

6 Make Temaki Sushi cones from the two lettuce leaves and fill them with sushi rice, carrot and radish strips, the beef fillet, and chives (see page 13).

7 Quarter the lemon slice and stick one piece in each cone. To ensure that the lettuce leaves stick together, wrap the lower part of the Temaki with strips of nori and tie them in a knot. Sprinkle the meat with the toasted sesame seeds. ■

For Enthusiasts & Initiates

Did you know that there is **sushi without any rice** and sushi served in a bowl with lots of rice and other ingredients. There is even a **steamed variety** of sushi that is quite common. So you see, the world of sushi is full of **exquisite surprises.**

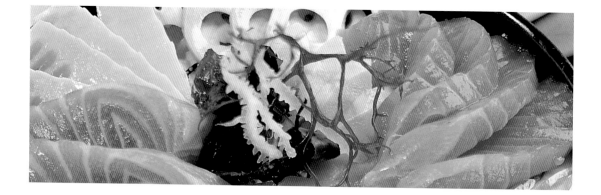

Food for the aesthete: Sashimi

Sashimi, a type of sushi without rice, consists of lean fish in its purest form, namely raw. It is neatly sliced or cut into strips that delicately melt on your tongue. In sushi bars—Japan's smallest culinary temples—sashimi is lovingly celebrated in picturesque arrangements with elaborate garnishes of finely chopped vegetables. Mixed sashimi is sometimes served with shrimp and salmon roe. The fish slices can sometimes pose quite a challenge to Western tastebuds but to the gourmet they are the highlight of every sushi meal. Sashimi is also suitable as an appetizer in a Western menu. You eat sashimi by dipping every bite in soy sauce that may also be seasoned with wasabi paste.

Sashimi's many variations

Almost every fish variety is suitable for the preparation of sashimi—as long as it is of the finest quality and as fresh as possible. Tuna sashimi is a favorite, as are marinated mackerel, halibut, sole, turbot, gilthead bream, scallops, and salmon. You can also prepare sashimi with freshwater fish such as trout or catfish. You combine the fish with seasoning ingredients such as paper-thin sliced white radish (daikon), thin scallion rings, finely grated ginger, or lemon slices. The Japanese serve sashimi in harmony with the seasons. A fish is used only when its flavor is a its best for the time of year. Thus cold water fish are said to taste best in fall or winter, whereas warm water fish have more flavor in the summer months.

Chirashi Sushi—A Far Eastern Delicacy

This variety originates in the far-eastern part of Japan and is particularly appreciated in Tokyo. Chirashi Sushi is one of the easiest to make. Each diner is served in a bowl containing warm sushi rice with various raw and cooked ingredients. The name means "scattered" sushi, which is misleading, however, as the ingredients are not just sprinkled at random over the rice but carefully and decoratively arranged.

In some Japanese provinces, the rice is combined with the ingredients. As there are so many combinations, the preparation is mainly dependent upon personal taste and preferences, less on set recipes. The rice used both for Chirashi Sushi and Mushi Sushi should be more highly seasoned than for other types of sushi, so use a little more rice vinegar and salt.

Savor the harmony of the ingredients

Chirashi Sushi is eaten with chopsticks—you can also use forks. A little of the ingredients are picked up with the rice and the mixture dipped in soy sauce. However, soy sauce is frequently sprinkled over the whole dish. It is important to have the mixture of ingredients and sushi rice on your tongue at the same time, so that you end up with the characteristic flavor.

Mushi Sushi—the hot alternative

Most of the sushi varieties are served at room temperature. Mushi Sushi, however, is a steamed sushi served hot at the table. It is prepared and arranged like Chirashi Sushi, the difference being that Mushi Sushi is then cooked over a steam bath for a short while. That is why it is often served in cold weather in Japan. This unusual variety of sushi will help you use leftovers from other meals, which can be warmed up and used in this way.

Steaming

You can arrange the respective ingredients in two or four bamboo steamer baskets (available in all Asian stores) which are stacked for steaming. If you don't have any such baskets, arrange the ingredients in four serving bowls or deep plates and place them on a flat sieve or trivet in the bottom of a steamer pot. Place a folded kitchen towel under the pot lid to prevent condensed water droplets from raining down on the food. If there's only room for two bowls or plates, steam the remaining sushi in another pot, or steam two portions at a time consecutively.

Sashimi with Sea-bass and Scallops

Serves Four • A bit more time-consuming • Particularly ornamental

Ingredients
4 oz seaweed (dulse)
2 oz white radish (daikon)
1 cucumber (about 4 in long)
14 oz fresh sea-bass fillet
8 scallops
1 lemon
4 tsp wasabi paste
2 toasted nori leaves
4 cooked shrimp in the shell
4 tbsp salmon roe

For dipping and accompaniments
soy sauce • Pickled ginger

Time *30 minutes*
125 calories per portion

1 Blanch the seaweed for two minutes. Refresh it in cold water and drain it.

2 Clean the radish, peel it, and slice it lengthwise into very thin strips. Wash the cucumber, halve it lengthwise, remove the seeds with a spoon, and cut the halves diagonally into thin slices.

3 Slice the sea bass fillet at an angle against the grain into slices just under ½ inch wide. Cut the scallop in thin slices.

4 Wash the lemon in hot water, dry it, and slice it thinly. Cut the nori sheets into strips. Peel the shrimp but do not cut off the tails.

5 Arrange the seaweed, the radish strips, cucumber slices, and fish strips together with the scallop slices and one shrimp each on each of the four flat dishes or sushi boards. Serve with 1 tablespoon wasabi paste, a few lemon slices, and nori strips , and 1 tablespoon salmon roe. ■

Sashimi with Oysters, Tuna, and Salmon

Serves four • Easy to prepare • A little more expensive

Ingredients
1 carrot
4 oz radish
1 dried chili pepper
7 oz very fresh salmon fillet
7 oz very fresh tuna fillet
8 oysters
1 lime
2 toasted nori sheets
4 tsp wasabi paste

For dipping and accompaniments
soy sauce • shredded pickled ginger

Time *30 minutes*
240 calories per portion

1 Clean, peel, and slice the carrots lengthwise into very thin strips.

2 Clean and peel the radish and carve a little hole in the center. Put the chili pepper inside it and grate the radish finely together with the chili. Squeeze the grated radish and shape it into four small balls.

3 Dry the salmon and tuna fillet with a cloth and slice diagonally, against the grain, in slices just under ½ inch thick.

Shuck the oysters and remove the flesh from the top shell leaving it in the lower shell.

4 Wash the lime in hot water, dry it, and slice it thinly. Cut the nori sheets into strips.

5 Arrange the carrot strips, the radish balls, salmon, and tuna strips together with the oysters, lime slices, wasabi paste, and the nori sheets decoratively on four platters or sushi boards. ■

Sashimi with
Sea-bass and Scallops

Sashimi with Oysters,
Tuna, and Salmon

Mixed Fish Sashimi

Serves Four • Allow plenty of time for preparation

Ingredients

For the marinated mackerel:
1 very fresh mackerel fillet
with skin (about 4 oz)
coarse salt
3 tbsp rice vinegar
1 tbsp mirin (Japanese
cooking sherry)
1 tsp sugar

Additionally:
2 tbsp dried seaweed (kaiso,
dulse, or wakame)
2 oz white radish (daikon)
½ carrot
2 oz cucumber or pickle
1 small untreated lemon
A few parsley leaves
4 oz fresh salmon and tuna
fillets
2 fresh scallops
4 cooked and peeled shrimp
(about 1 oz each)
3 tbsp salmon roe
2–4 toasted nori leaves
4 tsp wasabi paste

Time *1 hour (+ 4–5 hours*
resting time)
160 calories per portion

1 Remove any remaining fishbones from the mackerel fillets with tweezers and trim the ragged edges with a knife. Rub the fillet with a coarse salt on each side, wrap in clingfilm and let it rest for 4–5 hours in the refrigerator. Then rinse off the salt under running water. Dry the fish fillet with a cloth.

2 Put the mackerel fillet in a shallow bowl. Combine the rice vinegar, mirin, and sugar. Pour the marinade over the fish, cover it, and refrigerate it for at least 30 minutes or rather 1 hour, turning once in between. Some 30 minutes before serving, wash the seaweed. Put it in a bowl, cover with cold water, and soak for 15 minutes.

3 Clean and peel the radish and half a carrot. Cut both first into thin slices, then diagonally into very thin strips. Wash, dry, and cut the cucumber into thin slice. then cut them in half. Wash the lemon in cold water, dry it, and cut in thin slices. cut these in half. Wash and dry the parsley leaves with a cloth.

4 Remove the mackerel fillet from the marinade and dry it with a cloth. Remove the skin, starting at the tail end by detaching some skin with a knife. Hold the fish firmly with one hand and peel off the skin with the other. Cut the mackerel into fillets diagonally against the grain into slices about ½ inch thick.

5 Transfer the seaweed to a sieve and drain the water from it. Slice the tuna and salmon diagonally against the grain into slices less than ½ inch thick. Wash the white flesh of the scallops briefly, dry with a cloth, and cut in thin slices.

6 Arrange the fish and the scallops with salmon roe, vegetables, lemon juice, nori sheets, seaweed, parsley and wasabi paste on four wooden trenchers or flat ornamental dishes. ∎

Chirashi Sushi with Vegetables and Scrambled Egg

Serves Four • Vegetarian • Sophisticated

Ingredients

For the vegetables:
12 dried shiitake mush-
rooms
2 large carrots
2 tbsp sugar
6 tbsp soy sauce
4 tbsp mirin (Japanese
cooking sherry)
4 slices lotus root, bottled
3 oz pickled ginger
salt
1¾ cups sugar snap peas

For the scrambled egg:
6 eggs
2 tsp sugar
2 tsp salt
2 tsp soy sauce
8 tbsp sake (Japanese rice
wine)
1 tbsp butter

Additionally:
1 lb 5 oz–1 lb 12 oz warmed
prepared sushi rice (recipe
page 16)

Time *35 minutes (+ 20 min-*
utes resting time)
600 calories per portion

1 Pour 1½ cups boiling water over the dried mushrooms and soak for 20 minutes. Transfer to a fine sieve, collecting the soaking water. Rinse the mushrooms thoroughly and remove tough stems.

2 Clean, peel, and half the carrots lengthwise and then cut them diagonally. Bring the mushroom soaking water, sugar, soy sauce, and mirin to the boil. Simmer the mushrooms and the carrot halves for 10–12 minutes, stirring occasionally until the carrots are soft. Strain through a sieve, collecting the broth in a bowl. Slice the mushroom caps and carrots into strips. Place the vegetables and the broth in a warm place.

3 Drain the lotus roots and ginger. Bring salted water to the boil. Wash the sugar snap peas, and cook them in the salted water for three minutes or until al dente, adding the lotus roots in the last 30 seconds. Let the water drain off and refresh briefly in cold water. Cut the sugar snap peas lengthwise into strips, and reserve in a warm place together with the lotus roots.

4 To make the scrambled eggs, beat the eggs with the sugar, salt, soy sauce, and sake. Heat the butter in a nonstick pan, pour the egg mixture into it, and let it set, stirring occasionally, over low heat.

5 Divide the rice between four deep serving bowls. Sprinkle with a dash of the vegetable broth. Radiating in a star-shape, arrange the scrambled eggs, sugar snap peas, carrots, and mushrooms on the rice. Place a slice of lotus root, some pickled ginger, carrots, and sugar snap peas in the center as a garnish. ■

For enthusiasts and initiates

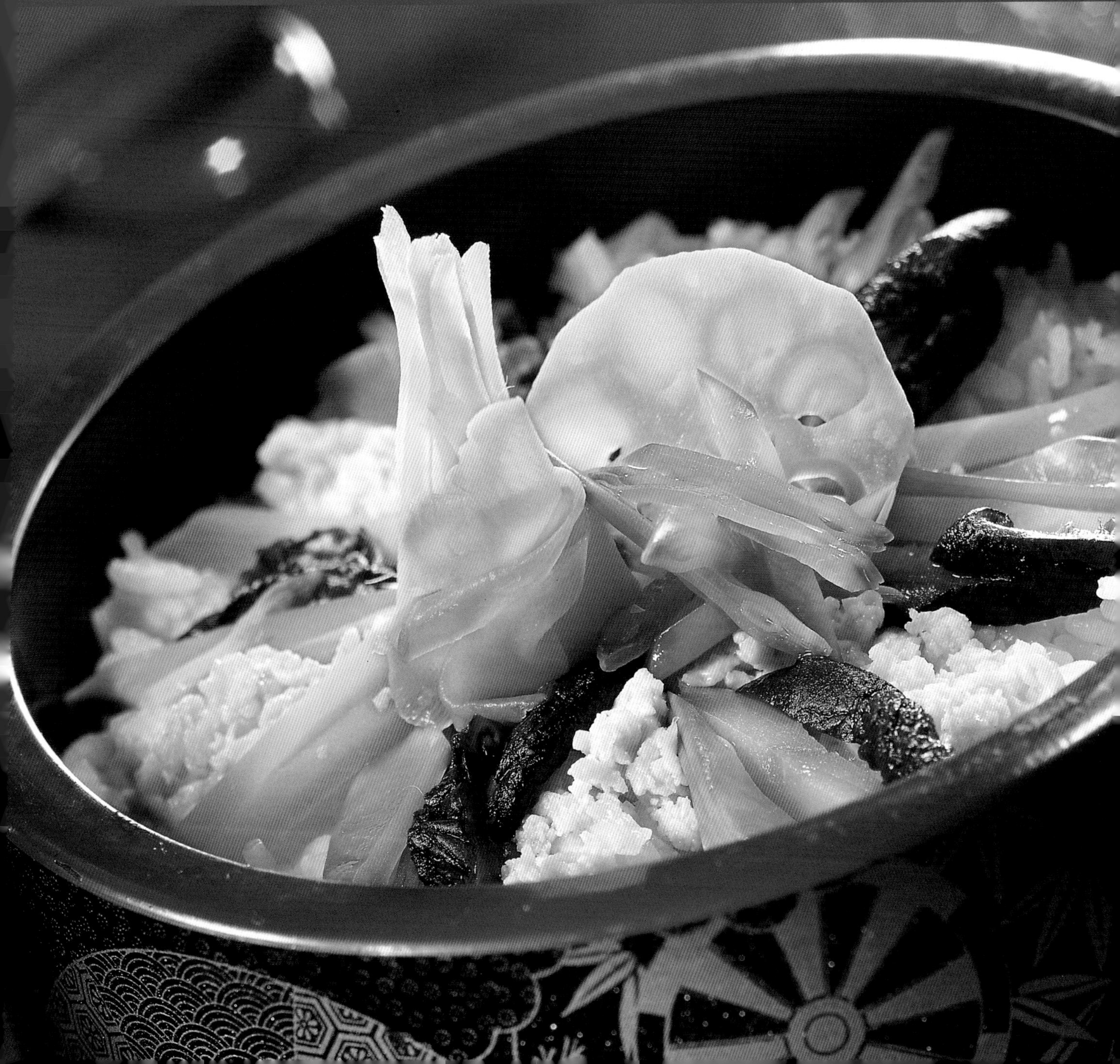

Chirashi Sushi with Mixed Fish

Serves four • For special occasions

Ingredients
½ oz dried pumpkin
1 tsp coarse salt
2 tsp sugar
2–3 tbsp soy sauce
2 tbsp mirin (Japanese
cooking sherry)
1 piece cucumber (about
2 in long)
2 oz white radish (daikon)
4 tsp wasabi paste
about 4 oz fresh salmon,
gilthead bream, and tuna
fillets
1 lb 5 oz–1 lb 12 oz warmed
prepared sushi rice (recipe
page 16)
4 cooked, peeled shrimp
(about 1 oz)
1 tbsp salmon roe
¼ cup pickled ginger

Time 40 minutes (+ 20 minutes soaking time)
450 calories per portion

1 Rinse the pumpkin briefly in water. Rub it in salt with your palms until soft-ened. Soak in warm water for at least 20 minutes. Drain and cover with fresh water, then simmer for 10 minutes, and drain again.

2 Return the pumpkin to the heat and cover with fresh water. Add sugar, soy sauce, and mirin. Simmer on low heat until almost all the water has evaporated. Pat the pumpkin dry and leave to cool.

3 While the pumpkin is cooking, wash the cucumber, dry it, and cut it at an acute angle into paper-thin slices. Halve these diagonally and cut out the core containing the seeds. Peel the radish and cut it lengthwise in very thin strips. Form the wasabi paste into four balls. Press down slightly and cut the surface into a star shape.

4 Dry the fish fillets with a cloth. Slice the salmon and tuna fillets diagonally against the grain in slices just under ½ inch wide. Cut the gilthead sea bream fillet the same way, into ¼-inch slices.

5 Divide the warmed sushi rice between four deep serving bowls. Decoratively arrange the salmon, tuna, and gilthead bream slices on it together with the shrimp, salmon roe, pumpkin, and radish strips, as well as the pickled ginger and the wasabi paste. ■

Ingredients

For the chili and sesame sauce:
1 tbsp soy sauce
1 tbsp sake (Japanese rice wine)
1 tbsp mirin (Japanese cooking sherry)
1 tbsp rice vinegar
1 tsp sesame oil
1 tsp chili oil
1 pinch Cayenne pepper
1 tbsp sesame seeds

Additionally:
300–400 g marbled beef fillet (trimmed of skin, fat, and sinews)
1½ tbsp sesame seeds
1 medium carrot, 1 small leek, 2 in white radish, and 2 in cucumber
salt
3 tbsp oil
600–800 g warm prepared sushi rice (recipe page 16)

Time 1 hour (+ resting overnight)
450 calories per portion

Chirashi Sushi with Lean Beef and Vegetables

Serves four • A little more expensive • Savory

1 Prepare the chili and sesame sauce the day before, by combining soy sauce, sake, mirin, rice vinegar, sesame, and chili oil as well as cayenne pepper in a bowl. Sprinkle with sesame seeds and leave covered overnight.

2 The following day, slice the beef fillet into four pieces around 1½ inch wide. Wrap them in aluminum foil and leave in the freezer for 45 minutes.

3 In the meantime, toast the sesame seeds in a dry pan until golden brown. Remove them and reserve them.

4 Wash and peel the vegetables. Cut into strips around 2 inches long and ¼ inch thick. Bring salted water to the boil. Blanch the carrot strips for two minutes, then add the leeks and cook for another minute. Drain both, refresh in cold water, drain again, cover, and set aside.

5 Strain the chili and sesame sauce through a fine sieve and discard the sesame seeds. Cut the semi-frozen beef fillet slices with a knife or meat slicer diagonally against the grain into even slices about ⅛ inch thick.

6 Heat the oil to a high temperature in a large pan. Sauté the slices of meat in batches for 1 minute, turning frequently. Return all the meat to the pan.

7 Add carrots, leeks, radish, and cucumber strips to the beef, as well as toasted sesame seeds and the chili and sesame sauce. Stir well to combine; add salt to taste. Cover and simmer for 1–2 minutes. Pour warm sushi rice into four deep bowls. Arrange the meat and vegetables decoratively on top. ■

Variation

Chirashi Sushi with pork

Use 10½–14 ounces lean pork, from the fillet or loin. Replace the leeks with three scallions and add a handful of soybean and mung bean sprouts. Prepare Chirashi Sushi as described in the recipe.

Ingredients

6 dried shiitake mushrooms
½ oz dried pumpkin
salt
1 tbsp sugar
3 tbsp soy sauce
2 tbsp mirin (Japanese
cooking sherry)
2 cups leaf spinach
¾ cup beansprouts
1 cup canned bamboo
shoots
4 raw peeled shrimp tails
(about ½-1 oz), fresh or
deep-frozen
⅓ cup rice vinegar
1 tsp sugar
6 oz very fresh salmon fillet
with skin
2–3 tbsp oil
1 lb 5 oz–1 lb 12 oz pre-
pared sushi rice (recipe
page 16)

Time 1½ hours
400 calories per portion

Steamed Sushi with Salmon and Shrimp

Serves four • Allow plenty of time for preparation

1 Pour ⅔ cup boiling water over the mushrooms and soak them for 20 minutes. In the meantime, rinse the pumpkin briefly in water. Rub it in 1 tablespoon salt between your palms until it is softer and rinse again. Soak in warm water at least for 20 minutes. Drain, cover with fresh water, and simmer for another 20 minutes; transfer to a sieve. Drain the mushrooms, collecting the soaking water in a bowl. Rinse the mushrooms thoroughly and remove the tough stems.

2 Bring the soaking water from the mushrooms with the sugar, soy sauce, and mirin to the boil. Remove immediately from the heat and leave to cool. Add the mushrooms and the pumpkin to the broth, return to the heat, and simmer, covered, for 15 minutes. Remove from the heat and leave to cool. Wash and trim the spinach. Blanch in salted water for 30 seconds. Drain and refresh in cold water, then drain again. Wash the bean sprouts and let them dry. Slice the bamboo shoots into slices about ⅛ inch thick.

3 Thread the fresh or thawed shrimp onto a skewer, ensuring that they do not shrivel up when cooking. Pour the rice vinegar into a pot with ½ cup water and the sugar and bring to the boil. Simmer the shrimp for three minutes. Remove, drain, and remove the skewers.

4 Pat the salmon fillet dry with a cloth and cut it into four slices. Sauté the slices in a nonstick pan in hot oil on medium heat for 30 seconds per side. Remove from the pan and sprinkle with a little salt.

5 Line two bamboo steamer baskets with aluminum foil, so that the foil is one inch above the rims. Fill each with half of the sushi rice. Arrange the prepared ingredients over the rice. Place the baskets on top of each other and cover the top one with a lid.

6 Pour 2 inches water into a steamer and place the baskets inside. They must not be allowed to touch the water. If necessary put a trivet in the bottom of the pot and place the baskets on top. Bring the water to the boil and steam the sushi on medium heat for 8–10 minutes. ■

Index

Credits

This edition published by
Barnes & Noble, Inc.,
by arrangement with
GRÄFE UND UNZER VERLAG
GmbH

2004 Barnes & Noble Books

© 2004 GRÄFE UND UNZER
VERLAG GmbH

M 10 9 8 7 6 5 4 3 2 1

ISBN 0-7607-5671-6

Production:
bookwise Medienproduktion
GmbH, Munich

Translation:
American Pie, London

Printed in China

Picture credits:
Barbara Bonisolli: 8, 9, 10 (steps),
11 (steps), 12 (steps), 13 (steps),
16 bottom, 17, 18–19, 23, 25, 27,
29, 31, 37, 38–39, 43, 45, 47, 49,
51, 53, 59, 60–61, 65, 67, 69, 73,
75, 77, 78–79

Michael Brauner: 7

Kai Mewes: 2, 3, 5, 6, 10 top,
11 top, 12 top and bottom, 13 top,
14, 15, 33, 40, 57, 62, 71, 80, 83, 96

Odette Teubner: cover, 4, 16 top
and middle, 20, 35, 55